PREDATORS
COBRAS

Barbara Taylor

Belitha Press

First published in the UK in 2003 by

Belitha Press
A member of Chrysalis Books plc
64 Brewery Road, London N7 9NT

Design and editorial production
Bender Richardson White
Copyright © Belitha Press 2002

ISBN 1 84138 670 7

British Library Cataloguing in Publication Data for this book is available from the British Library.

10 9 8 7 6 5 4 3 2 1

Acknowledgements
We wish to thank the following individuals and organizations for their help and assistance and for supplying material in their collections:
CORBIS Corporation/Images: pages 13 top (Joe McDonald), 18 (Tom Brakefield); 25 right (Keren Su); 27 (Christine Kolisch); 29 (Bojan Brecelj). Gallo Images/Anthony Bannister Photo Library: pages 6, 12, 23 bottom; pages 2, 10 (Daryl Balfour); 3, 17 bottom (Nigel J. Dennis); 5, 7 top, 8, 8–9, 30, 31 (Rod Patterson); 9 (Tim Jackson); 11 top, 17 top (Peter Lillie); 20 (Lex Hes); 23 top (Dirk Heinrich); 25 left (Keith Begg); 28 Robert C. Nunnington. Frank Lane Photo Agency: pages 11 bottom (Jurgen & Christine Sohns); 19 bottom (M. Ranjit); 26 (Michael Gore). Natural History Photo Agency: pages 4 (Hellio & Van Ingen); 1, 4–5, 16, 19 top, 21 top and bottom, 22, 24 (Daniel Heuclin); 13 (Pavel German); 15 (Andy Rouse). Ecoscene/Papilio: pages 7 bottom (Robert Pickett); 14 (Clive Druett).

Editorial Manager: Joyce Bentley
Assistant Editor: Clare Chambers
Project Editor: Lionel Bender
Text Editor: Kate Phelps
Design and Make-up: Ben White
Picture Research: Cathy Stastny
Consultant: John Stidworthy

Printed in Hong Kong

LOOK FOR THE PREDATOR

Look for the cobra in boxes like this. Here you will find extra facts, stories and other interesting information about cobras.

▼ A cobra hunts for prey among the branches of a tree (see page 10).

CONTENTS

▼ Cobras can move fast through desert grasses (see page 17).

WHAT ARE COBRAS?

Cobras are very poisonous snakes, famous for their deadly bite. They use their poison, which is called venom, to stun their prey or to defend themselves against predators, such as mongooses.

Cobras are members of the Elapid family of snakes, which all have short fangs fixed at the front of the mouth in the top jaw. There are more than 270 different kinds of cobras and their relatives in the Elapid family.

◀ Cobras are recognized by the hood on their neck, which they spread out when they are angry or disturbed. This is an Indian cobra.

Snakes belong to a group of animals called reptiles, which are covered in tough, waterproof scales that overlap like tiles on a roof. A snake's scales are extra-thick pieces of skin, which are made of keratin – the same material as your fingernails. Several times a year, snakes shed their old skin to reveal a bright, shiny new skin underneath.

All snakes are predators, or hunters, that eat prey such as lizards, rats, birds, fish – and other snakes! As reptiles they lay eggs, although some sea snakes give birth to live young. Snakes can live for up to 30 years.

COBRA FAMILY
The Elapid family includes the mambas, the coral snakes, the kraits and the many Australian snakes, including the taipan and the Tiger snake. Many sea snakes are also in the Elapid snake family.

▶ Cobras can lift up the front part of their body to look for danger or to appear more threatening.

◀ A Sea krait glides through the water in S-shaped curves searching for fish to eat. Its flattened tail works like the oar on a rowing boat to push it along.

KILLING MACHINE

A cobra's body is a long, thin tube, which is dry, not slimy, to the touch. It has no legs, so it wriggles, slithers and slides along. It does not have horns, spikes or body armour for protection, although its scales do help to protect its soft body.

What a cobra does have is poisonous venom. This helps it to kill its prey quickly, without having to fight a long battle in which it might be injured. All the important parts of a cobra are in the head end. The tongue flicks in and out to taste and smell the air. The eyes watch all around, and the ears inside the head pick up quiet sounds.

▼ The King cobra has a long, narrow hood, without patterns of any kind, unlike true cobras. Its smooth scales help it to slide along quickly as it chases its prey.

▲ Cobras have a slender body, a long tail, large eyes and a tendency to lift their head off the ground to search for prey. These are all characteristics of active hunters.

◄ A cobra's hood is made from flaps of skin supported by long ribs. The white circle on a Monocled cobra's hood looks like a big eye. This helps to distract predators or frighten them away.

The rest of the body contains long, thin organs such as the heart, lungs, kidneys and liver. The stomach and gut are very stretchy so they can hold large meals. This means the cobra can eat as much as possible at each meal, which is important because there may be gaps of several months between meals.

WHERE COBRAS LIVE

Cobras and their relatives are commonly found in hot, tropical places because they rely on heat from their surroundings to warm them up. In cool weather, cobras slow down and even become dormant, only stirring when the temperature rises.

Cobras are found in Africa, southern Asia and Australia. Their relatives, the coral snakes, live in America. Snakes in the cobra family live in forests, grasslands, scrub, deserts, swamps and the sea. They also live in and near villages and other settlements. The place where an animal lives is called its habitat.

▼ The Egyptian cobra is especially common near oases and human settlements. It feeds largely on lizards and sometimes lives in lizards' burrows.

▶ The Cape cobra from southern Africa lives in dry, scrubland habitats like this.

ALARMING AUSTRALIA

In most parts of the world, the number of snakes belonging to the cobra family is fairly small. But in Australia, cobras and their relatives make up 60 per cent of snakes. This is the only place in the world where poisonous snakes outnumber the harmless ones.

Most land-based cobras live on the ground, but in Africa there are cobras and mambas that live mostly in trees. The King cobras of Asia are good at climbing trees as well as being excellent swimmers. They often live near rainforest streams, where the temperature and humidity are relatively constant.

▼ A Cape cobra sticks its head out of the sand in the Kalahari desert. Only a few cobras live underground but many shelter in holes and crevices.

9

COBRA FOOD

Cobras eat a lot of other snakes and large lizards but also feed on frogs, birds and small mammals, such as rats and mice. They are often found near human settlements because there are plenty of rats to eat. Sea snakes and water cobras prefer fishy prey.

WHEN IS A WORM NOT A WORM?

The Australian Death adder has a brightly coloured tip to its tail that looks like a worm. It wriggles this 'worm' to lure lizards, birds and small mammals within reach of its deadly poisonous fangs.

▼ Cobras usually hunt on the ground but some climb trees in search of prey.

King cobras eat mainly other snakes. They usually prey on non-venomous snakes, for example Asian rat snakes and pythons, but will also eat highly poisonous snakes such as Indian cobras, kraits and even smaller King cobras. King cobras seem to be immune to the venom of their poisonous prey. Strange as it may seem, the King cobra will often share its sleeping-quarters with potential prey!

Baby cobras are ready to hunt after they first moult their skin at about a week old. They have fully formed fangs and venom glands, and their venom is just as strong as an adult's venom. But baby cobras cannot eat as big prey as their parents. However, in proportion to their size, snakes eat bigger meals than any other predator on land.

▲ A Cape cobra searching a bird's nest for baby birds to eat.

▼ Rat snakes are typical prey for snakes in the cobra family.

FANGS AND POISONS

A cobra's main weapons are its two venomous fangs, which are extra large teeth with sharp points on the end. These teeth are fixed to the top jaw and cannot move. A cobra's fangs are about 10 mm long.

If the fangs were any longer, the snake would bite through its lower jaw. Snakes in the viper family have longer fangs, but these can be folded back against the roof of the mouth. A snake's fangs are hollow and linked to bags of venom in the head, behind the eyes. The venom bags are special glands that in many other animals produce saliva, a juice that helps digest food. The venom itself is a clear, pale yellow fluid. As the venom is used up, the snake makes more, so it never runs out. Cobras are immune to their own venom.

DEADLY VENOM

The venom in one bite from an Australian Taipan snake is enough to kill up to 12 000 guinea pigs. The Fierce snake, or Inland taipan, is perhaps the most toxic venom of any snake. The venom in just one bite of this snake would be enough to kill more than 100 people or 250 000 mice!

▶ A South African rinkhal, a Spitting cobra, in an attacking pose, about to strike its prey.

▲ This skull of a King cobra shows the large fangs in the upper jaw. The jaws open very wide to swallow prey whole.

Behind the fangs and in the lower jaw, cobras have short, sharp teeth that curve backwards. These are good for gripping and holding prey; a cobra does not have any chewing teeth. None of the teeth are strong and often get broken, so they are continually being replaced. New fangs move into place before the old ones are lost, so that a snake may have two fangs on each side of its jaw for a short time.

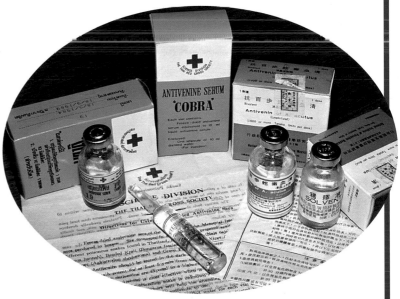

▲ Antivenin injected into a person's bloodstream neutralizes a cobra's poisonous venom.

COBRA SENSES

The most important senses for cobras and most other snakes are smell and taste. They do not rely as much on sight and hearing as we do. Snakes are almost the only animals to taste and smell with their tongues.

In the roof of a snake's mouth is an organ called the Jacobson's organ, which analyses tastes and smells collected by the tongue. It opens into the mouth by two small holes, like nostrils. The snake presses one fork of its tongue into each opening, which is why snakes have a forked tongue.

A snake's eyes are always wide open because they do not have any eyelids. Snakes cannot blink or close their eyes. Each eye is protected by a transparent scale called a spectacle. It is difficult to know if snakes can see colours, but there is evidence that at least some of them can.

▼ King cobras appear to be more intelligent than other cobras. Zookeepers say they learn faster than other snakes and can tell their keepers apart from strangers.

▶ A snake's forked tongue collects chemicals from the air to find out about food, mates, predators and any other interesting things happening nearby. The tongue is not a sting. A snake can put out its tongue without opening its mouth, through a small notch in its upper jaw.

GOOD VIBRATIONS

Many people think that snakes are deaf, but they do have one ear bone joined to the jaw. They can pick up sound vibrations through the ground and probably some low sounds travelling through the air.

GOING HUNTING

Cobras are active hunters that chase their prey rather than lying in wait to ambush it. They hunt mainly by smell, 'tasting' the air with their forked tongues.

Cobras track their prey carefully to get as close as possible. They slither and slide along the ground or the branch of a tree, or wriggle through the water, until they are a few inches away. Then they attack with a rush. They strike with their fangs and overcome their prey with a massive dose of venom.

NEW SPECTACLES

King cobras may see clearly up to 100 metres (300 feet) away but they do not rely on sight when hunting. This is just as well because when they shed their skin, they suffer from poor eyesight for up to 10 days while new eye coverings (like contact lenses) form.

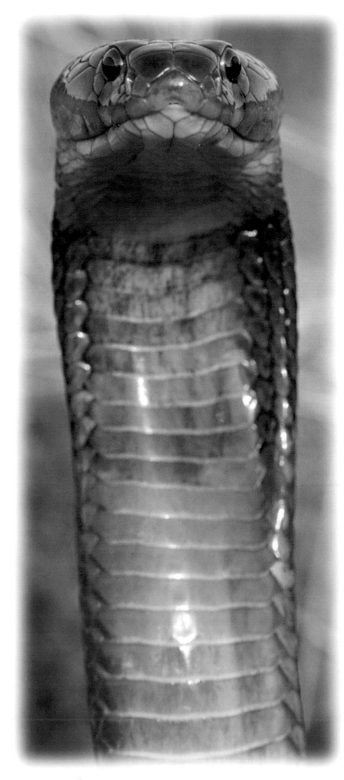

▶ Cobras get very near to their prey and only rely on eyesight for the final approach.

Most cobras hunt in the evening but they will also hunt during the day. The King cobra's round pupils let in lots of light, which is useful when it hunts in daylight. Nocturnal snakes, which only hunt at night, usually have vertical pupils because these can be closed more tightly than a circular pupil during the day. This protects the snake's sensitive eyes from bright light during the day.

▲ An African Cape cobra glides towards the nest of sociable weaver birds, which build huge thatched nests in trees.

▼ Cobras can chase their prey for some distance, moving forwards rapidly with the head raised off the ground.

IN FOR THE KILL

When a cobra closes in for the kill, it raises its body and strikes straight down, usually making a sharp hissing sound. Its fangs pierce the victim's skin and it pumps venom down the hollow fangs and into the victim's body.

Cobras tend to hang on to their prey with their teeth until they are sure enough poison has entered the wound. The longer the snake bites or the deeper it bites, the more venom is injected.

ROYAL DEATH

A King cobra's venom is less toxic than a Common cobra's. But a King cobra delivers more venom with each bite – enough to kill an elephant or 20 people. The King cobra causes only about five human deaths a year – rattlesnakes in North America kill about 25 people a year.

▼An Egyptian Banded cobra slides through the grass towards it's prey.

Cobra venom contains a mixture of poisons.
Most of the poisons cause breathing or heart problems,
or paralysis. This keeps the prey still while the snake swallows
its meal. Other poisons start digesting the paralysed victim.

Cobras have no limbs to tear food and their teeth cannot chop
and chew food into smaller pieces. So they gulp down every
meal whole. Special loose jaws allow the snake to open its
mouth really wide. Then the jaws 'walk' from side to side over
the food to force it down the snake's throat.

▲This cobra is a
cannibal because it is
eating another cobra of
its own kind. It may
take several days or
even weeks to digest
its meal.

▶ Snakes are easy for
King cobras to swallow
because they slide
down the throat easily.
A snake can usually
swallow its prey in
10 to 20 minutes,
although an extra-
large meal may take
an hour to swallow.

COLOUR AND CAMOUFLAGE

The colours of cobras and other snakes come from pigments inside the scales and the way light reflects off the scales. When a snake's skin is stretched, such as by a cobra spreading its hood, the scales pull apart so you can see the skin between the scales. The skin may be a different colour from the scales.

Typical cobras have mottled brown, black and sandy colours that make them difficult to see, especially when they hide under bushes or in the undergrowth. In forests, King cobras have darker skins and in open forests or on plains, they have lighter skins. These camouflage colours help them to hide from prey or enemies.

FALSE COLOURS
Milk snakes and false coral snakes are not poisonous but they copy the warning colours of coral snakes. Predators leave them alone too, rather than risk being bitten.

◄ The colours and patterns of the Egyptian cobra are hard to spot among the dry grass and rocks where it lives.

▶ A Gold cobra becomes hard to see against the dry desert grass.

Some members of the cobra family, such as kraits and coral snakes, are striped with much brighter colours. These stripes warn predators to leave the snakes alone because they are deadly poisonous. They are called warning colours.

▶ Most kraits have bold black-and-white or black-and-yellow stripes to warn that their venom is very toxic. Kraits come out at night and feed mainly on other snakes.

SELF-DEFENCE

Cobras have many enemies, such as mongooses and people. Wild boar and mongooses steal cobra eggs, and baby cobras may be eaten by army ants, giant centipedes and civet cats.

Cobras usually try to escape enemies by keeping still or crawling under rocks or into a hole. But if they have to fight, cobras rear up and spread the hood wide to scare enemies away. The huge hood also makes a cobra look too big for an enemy to swallow. Cobras only bite as a last resort, if they fail to scare a predator. Mambas have no hood, but they can inflate their throat instead.

Cobras may also hiss loudly to make themselves even more frightening. The hiss is produced by air passing through tiny holes in the snake's windpipe. A King cobra's hiss sounds rather like a dog growling.

▼ Mongooses usually win fights with cobras because of their speed, agility and timing. Cobras are slower than many snakes and the mongoose's thick coat helps to protect it against the snake's fangs.

◀ A Western Black spitting cobra defending its eggs. Unless they are defending their eggs or young, cobras are more likely to slither away than attack.

Several African cobras do more than hiss and show a scary hood. They spray venom through small slits at the tips of their fangs. They only spit venom to defend themselves and give themselves time to escape, not to catch prey. One spitting cobra, the rinkhals, will even "play dead" at first, since predators prefer live prey and may leave it alone. If this does not work, it will come back to life and spit venom instead.

SUPER SPIT
A spitting cobra can spray its venom more than 2 m. It aims directly into an attacker's eyes and its aim is deadly accurate.

▶ Venom streaming from a Spitting cobra's fangs. If venom gets in the eyes, it causes a burning pain and blindness that may last for several hours or even be permanent.

UNDER THREAT

The biggest threat to cobras and other snakes comes from people, who often kill the reptiles through fear and ignorance.

People build houses and farms on land where snakes live. Snakes are often killed by vehicles on roads, for meat or for sport. Farmers kill snakes to protect their farm animals and workers, although cobras and other snakes can help farmers by eating pests.

▼ An Indian cobra being captured by people who are trying to protect their village and animals.

In some countries, snakes are killed so parts of their bodies, such as their skin, meat and bile, can be used in Chinese medicines. Cobras are killed for their beautiful skins, which are made into belts, purses, shoes and other luxury items. In one year, more than ten million snakes were killed in India for the skin industry.

To help cobras and other snakes to survive, people need to learn more about them and take action to preserve their habitats. Snakes and people do not mix well together so the snakes need undisturbed habitats well away from people where they can live and hunt in their natural environment.

COBRA KILLERS

In India, about 10 000 people a year die from snakebites, mostly from the bites of the Spectacled cobra. About 10 per cent of cobra bites kill people, when antivenin is not available.

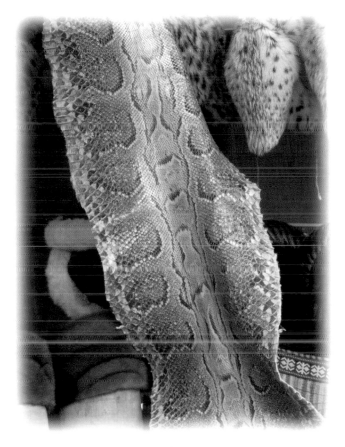

▲ Snake skins are traded illegally and tourists caught bringing them back from holidays can be heavily fined. This is a python skin.

◀ Cobras are beautiful, shy, secretive snakes that are not as dangerous as people think. They will not usually attack people unless they feel threatened.

COBRA FACTS

Here is a selection of interesting facts and figures about cobras.

FIRST SNAKES

The first snakes appeared between 100 and 150 million years ago, alongside the dinosaurs. The cobra family did not evolve until the Miocene Period, which lasted from 22.5 million to 5.5 million years ago. Nowadays, there are some 2,700 different kinds of snake but less than a quarter of them are poisonous. Only 300 of these poisonous snakes, including members of the cobra family, are able to kill people.

WORSHIPPING COBRAS

The cobra symbol has been found on seals in the ruins of Mohenjo-Daro, in southern Pakistan, an ancient city about 4000 years old. In India, the cobra has been widely worshipped since ancient times. Hindu mythology depicts a cobra-race called Nagas, who inhabit the underworld, Nagalok or Patala. Manasa or Durgamma, queen of the Nagas, is worshipped by women to protect their children from snakebites. On the Hindu festival of Nagapanchami, people pour milk and even blood on images of cobras and down snake holes. King cobras have also been worshipped as Sun gods, with the power over rain, thunder and fertility.

◀ Snake charmers do not really hypnotize cobras with their flute music. Instead the cobra follows the movements of the pipe, swaying from side to side. Often the snakes are exhausted or have had their fangs removed.

CREATION COBRAS

A Hindu creation myth describes a gigantic cobra called Shesha which sheltered the god Vishnu. Shesha had from five to 1000 heads. When Shesha yawned, massive earthquakes happened and fire from his mouths or his venom destroyed the world.

COBRAS IN THE MOVIES

The cobra is also a very popular theme in Indian films. Usually, the cobra is shown as a guardian of goodness and a destroyer of the wicked. Many films are based on the myth of the Icchadari cobras, which are said to have the power to take on a human form and have one devoted mate. If the mate is killed, the cobra is able to see the image of the killer in the dead snake's eyes and sets off on a trail of revenge.

COMFORTING COBRAS

The African Leitayo tribe will never kill a cobra because they believe that a cobra will comfort a woman about to give birth. The cobra is supposed to stay with the woman until a day after the child is born to see that all is well. It is then given milk to drink, after which it leaves. The Leitayo maintain that cobras are members of their tribe and so will not harm tribefolk.

CLEOPATRA'S COBRA

The Egyptian cobra is famous for being the asp that Queen Cleopatra of ancient Egypt used to commit suicide. It is likely that Cleopatra chose this snake because it has a quick-acting venom. A real asp is just as poisonous, but causes a slow and painful death.

▼ A Buddhist story describes how a massive cobra spread its hood over the Buddha to protect him from the Sun while he meditated. Cobra images guard the entrances of many Buddhist and Hindu temples.

COBRA WORDS

This glossary explains some of the words used in this book that you might not have seen before.

Antivenin
is a medicine used to treat a snakebite. It is made by injecting a horse (or other mammal) with treated snake venom so the horse's blood produces antibodies against the venom.

Cannibal
an animal that eats others of its species or type.

Camouflage
colours or patterns that allow a snake to blend in with its surroundings.

Cold-blooded
an animal whose temperature varies with that of its surroundings.

Cobras
poisonous snakes in the Elapid family, with short, fixed fangs at the front of the mouth.

Dormant period
a resting period when an animal's or a plant's body shuts down to help it survive harsh times.

◀ An Egyptian cobra with an extended hood.

Elapids
a group of poisonous snakes that includes cobras, mambas, coral snakes, sea snakes, kraits and many Australian snakes.

Evolve
to develop into a variety of different species over long periods of time, in response to changes in the environment.

Fang
a long, pointed tooth, which may be used to deliver venom.

Habitat
the place where an animal or a plant lives.

Hood
skin behind a cobra's head that opens out to frighten enemies.

Jacobson's organ
nerve pits in the roof of a snake's mouth into which the snake places its tongue. The pits can identify chemicals on the tongue.

Keratin

a horny substance that a snake's scales are made of.

Moult

to cast off a layer of dead skin.

Pigment

colouring matter.

Predator

an animal that hunts other animals and eats them.

Prey

an animal that is hunted and killed by another animal – a predator – for food.

Pupil

the area in the middle of the front of the eye through which light enters.

Reptile

a cold-blooded animal with a bony skeleton and a scaly skin. Reptiles lay eggs or give birth to live young. They usually live on land.

Salivary gland

a gland in the mouth that produces a colourless liquid

◄ The Egyptian cobra's raised head and inflated hood was often depicted on the headdresses of Ancient Egyptian pharaohs. This was the symbol of the goddess Ejo. The Egyptians associated snakes with rain, fertility and wealth.

called saliva. This helps food to slide down the throat and contains digestive juices.

Scale

small, overlapping plates that grow out of the top layer of a reptile's skin and help to protect it.

Spectacle

a see-through scale that covers a snake's eye.

Venom

poisonous fluid produced by some snakes to kill their prey and defend themselves from

enemies. Venom is injected into prey by biting.

Vipers

a group of poisonous snakes with fangs which fold back against the roof of the mouth.

Warning colours

bright colours – mostly as stripes – that warn of an animal's poisonous nature.

Windpipe

the pipe that leads from the throat to the lungs, through which air enters and leaves the lungs.

COBRA PROJECTS

If you want to find out more about cobras, here are some ideas for projects.

WATCHING COBRAS

The best places to watch cobras and other snakes close up are zoos and wildlife centres. There may be demonstrations where experienced animal handlers allow you to touch and hold snakes that are not dangerous. You could take photographs or draw sketches and make notes about things such as where the snakes come from and what they eat. Look out for articles in newspapers or magazines and build up a snake file with all the information you have collected.

WHAT EATS WHAT?

Starting with an African cobra, draw a food chain for wildlife on the grasslands of Africa. A food chain is a diagram linking each animal with the animals or plants it feeds on. The text in this book will give you some of the 'links' in the cobras' chain. To find more links, look at other books in your local library or at some of the internet sites listed opposite. See how many links you can make.

▲ A Cape cobra spreads its hood in a threat display. The hood makes it look bigger and more dangerous.

◀ A South African cobra, a member of the most venomous snake family.

COBRAS ON THE WEB
If you have access to the Internet, try looking up these websites.

www.cobras.org
A good general site, with lots of information about cobras and links to other sites.

www.nationalgeographic.com/features/ 97/kingcobra/index-n.html
Information about the King cobra and its lifestyle, with amazing pictures, such as: venom dripping off the fangs, the tongue flicking in and out, the snake hissing and eating, and much more.

www.creatures2.animallovers.co.uk/ kingcobra.html
Information about the distribution, size, lifestyle, food, breeding, conservation and breeding of this very special snake.

www.worldalmanacforkids.com/explore/ animals/snake.html
General information about all snakes, such as habitats, movement, physical characteristics, behaviour and reproduction.

Other sites that feature a variety of wildlife including cobras:
animal.discovery.com/fansites/jeffcorwin/ carnival/slithering/blackmamba.html

animaldiversity.ummz.umich.edu/chordata/ reptilia/squamata/elapidae.html

www.bbc.co.uk/nature

HOW YOU CAN HELP
Join a conservation group to find out more about snakes and other reptiles and see how you can help snakes survive in the future. Many zoos and conservation groups have schemes which allow you to sponsor or adopt rare snakes and help to pay for their upkeep.

INDEX